LET'S GET A PET!

MY FIRST DOG

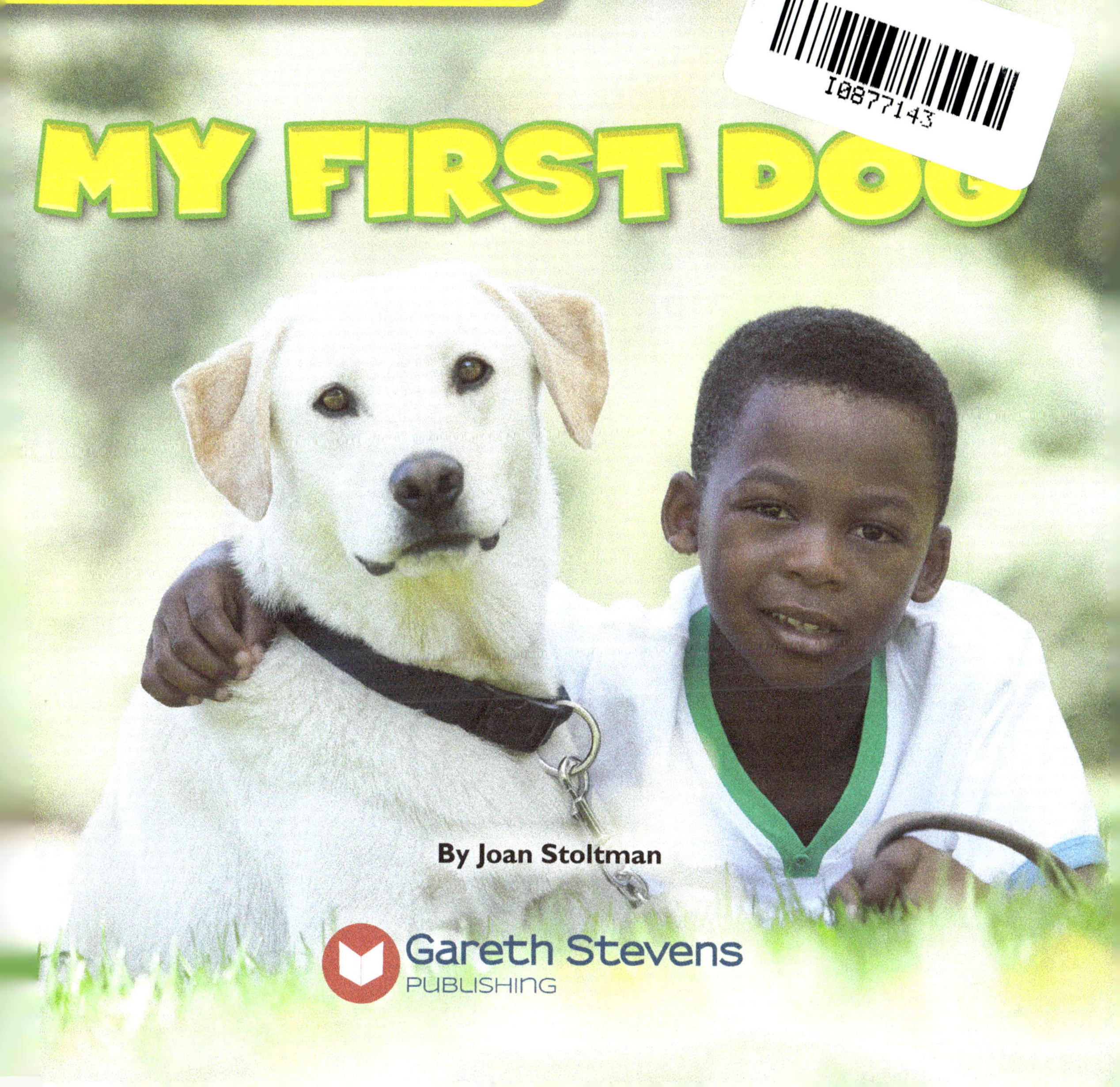

By Joan Stoltman

Gareth Stevens
PUBLISHING

Please visit our website, www.garethstevens.com. For a free color catalog of all our high-quality books, call toll free 1-800-542-2595 or fax 1-877-542-2596.

Cataloging-in-Publication Data

Names: Stoltman, Joan.
Title: My first dog / Joan Stoltman.
Description: New York : Gareth Stevens Publishing, 2018. | Series: Let's get a pet! | Includes index.
Identifiers: ISBN 9781482464498 (pbk.) | ISBN 9781482464511 (library bound) | ISBN 9781482464504 (6 pack)
Subjects: LCSH: Dogs–Juvenile literature.
Classification: LCC SF426.5 S76 2017 | DDC 636.7–dc23

Published in 2018 by
Gareth Stevens Publishing
111 East 14th Street, Suite 349
New York, NY 10003

Designer: Bethany Perl
Editor: Joan Stoltman

Photo credits: Cover, p. 1 wavebreakmedia/Shutterstock.com; pp. 2–24 (background texture) Liliya Mulyukova/Shutterstock.com; p. 5 bbernard/Shutterstock.com; p. 7 belu gheorghe/ Shutterstock.com; p. 9 SomPhoto/Shutterstock.com; p. 11 CLS Digital Arts/Shutterstock.com; p. 13 (dog bowl) Africa Studio/Shutterstock.com; p. 13 (dog bed) boytsov/Shutterstock.com; p. 13 (main image) Giedriusok/Shutterstock.com; p. 15 Vladislav Gajic/Shutterstock.com; p. 17 vvvita/Shutterstock.com; p. 19 bepsy/Shutterstock.com; p. 21 (black labrador) Erik Lam/ Shutterstock.com; p. 21 (golden retriever) Irina oxilixo Danilova/Shutterstock.com; p. 21 (poodle) Jagodka/Shutterstock.com; p. 21 (chihuahua) Eric Isselee.

Printed in the United States of America

CPSIA compliance information: Batch #CS17GS: For further information contact Gareth Stevens, New York, New York at 1-800-542-2595.

CONTENTS

Boldface words appear in the glossary.

Dogs Are Great!

There are many different kinds of dogs, and they're all pretty smart! Since dogs are **pack** animals like coyotes and wolves, they'll think of your family as their pack. This means they'll form strong friendships—that's why they're known as "man's best friend"!

Amazing Dogs!

There are more than 400 breeds, or kinds, of dogs. Dogs can be as little as 4 inches (10 cm) tall or as much as 44 inches (112 cm) tall! They **pant** to cool themselves off. Dogs even dream, just like we do!

Dogs can hear four times better and smell at least 10,000 times better than people! In fact, their sense of smell is so good they can follow the smell of a person or object for many miles. That's why they're used for hunting and for finding missing people!

Dogs can see in the dark! Plus, because their eyes are far apart, they see really far to the left and right. It's believed dogs see in blue, yellow, green, and gray. A dog's noseprint is one of a kind, like a snowflake or fingerprint!

NOSE

What a Dog Needs

A new home is both exciting and **stressful** for a dog. Help them get used to a new **schedule** of meals, walks, and playtime so they can get comfortable. Also, dogs sleep half the day, so they need a warm, quiet, soft place to rest.

WATER BOWL
FOOD BOWL
LEASH
DOG BED

If a dog's schedule isn't kept, they can get stressed. They might chew things they aren't supposed to or pee inside. You can help by giving weekly brushings, cleaning up poop in the yard, taking them on walks, and helping with meals!

BRUSH

Train That Pup!

Training means teaching a dog to sit, come, and more. Training helps your dog and family get along and **communicate**. Hitting and yelling don't teach dogs good **behavior**. It's best if you give your dog treats when they do well and practice often!

Walking

Dogs need a walk at least once daily. Always have a collar with an **ID** and a leash on your dog! Dogs greet one another by smelling each other. They'll want to do this to people, so teach them to "stay" during training!

Canine Communication

Dogs communicate using their ears, eyes, tail, voice, and mouth. Pay attention! What does your dog do when you're playing, saying "sit," or coming home? Watch carefully, and you'll soon know a lot about what your dog is thinking!

KINDS OF DOGS

GOLDEN RETRIEVER

CHIHUAHUA

BLACK LABRADOR

POODLE

GLOSSARY

behavior: the way an animal acts

communicate: to let someone know how you're feeling and what you're thinking

ID: short for "identification," or the tag that should have the dog's name and owner's address and phone number on it

pack: a group like a family that does everything together, such as hunting and sleeping

pant: when a dog breathes loudly and quickly with their tongue out

schedule: doing the same things at the same time every day

stressful: full of stress, or a feeling of worry

FOR MORE INFORMATION

BOOKS

Barnes, Julia. *Puppies*. Broomall, PA: Mason Crest, 2017.

Bluemel Oldfield, Dawn. *Dog*. New York, NY: Bearport Publishing, 2017.

Martin, Ann M. *Because of Shoe and Other Dog Stories*. New York, NY: Henry Holt, 2012.

WEBSITES

Dog Games
pbskids.org/games/dog/
Play over 16 different online dog video games!

How to Love Your Dog: A Kid's Guide to Dog Care
www.loveyourdog.com/
Learn all about how to care for your new dog!

List of Dog Movies
www.ducksters.com/moviesforkids/list_of_dog_movies_for_kids.php
Check out these great dog movies at your local library!

Publisher's note to educators and parents: Our editors have carefully reviewed these websites to ensure that they are suitable for students. Many websites change frequently, however, and we cannot guarantee that a site's future contents will continue to meet our high standards of quality and educational value. Be advised that students should be closely supervised whenever they access the Internet.

INDEX